THE FOREST

T.C. ANDERSON

the forest

```
01001110 01101111 01110100 01101000 01101001
01101110 01100111 00100000 01100111 01110010
01101111 01110111 01110011 00101100 00100000
01100010 01110101 01110100 00100000 01100101
01110110 01100101 01110010 01111001 01110100
01101000 01101001 01101110 01100111 00100000
01101100 01101001 01110110 01100101 01110011
00100000 01101001 01101110 00100000 01000010
01110010 01100101 01100001 01101011 01110111
         01100001 01110100 01100101 01110010
```

The Forest

First Printing, 2021
Printing information available on the last page.

ISBN 978-1-0879-2411-3 (sc)
ISBN 978-1-0879-2412-0 (e)[1]

Project Manager: Beth Huston
Creative Director: Tricia Jones
Riza Publishing Press
www.rizapress.com

FOR JARED,

my king volcano.

INTRO

Read me like a dictionary
of the life I once lived.
Tear and crease my paper
like leaves of silk on a
swaying branch.
Seek me deeply
like my thirsty,
labrynthine roots.
Climb my limbs like
unclaimed history.
See these pages as they lay
before you:
a forest of infinite stories.

ACT I

the branches

FALL IN AND FEEL FREE

Are we really dead?
Are we really alive?

We come into this world
on our deathbeds,
books full of memories,
filtered through the
world's microscope.

How have you fared in this weary world?
Are you really listening?

Fall in and feel free.

DRINK FROM YOUR BONES

Imagine what we could become.

A storm
        of many colors,
        on time and
        in motion,
        calm and
        mild and
        sedate and
        smooth.

Pain in the knuckles,
passion in the heart,
the chains that
        rattle and
        bind
        untethered from the world.

When the wind tousles,
        streaks of amber
        'midst the blue,
I drink from your bones.

STRINGS THAT BIND

Strings that bind the world,

we
   trip
      over
         our
            own

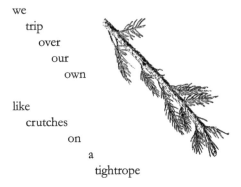

like
   crutches
         on
           a
           tightrope

Blinded by fairy tales and white knights
         (uncanny, with a hint of whimsy),
each lie a cog in the
       machine of the world...

The egg never fell off the wall.

SPLIT YOU INTO ASHES

Oh, how I'd love to
split you into ashes.

I feel your beautiful pieces,
the warmth of you,
your uncomplicated secrets.

The sound of the dying,
careful and quiet,
calls to me.

Split the skin,
you monster made human.
Swallow hungrily,
find me in your veins…

If only you had listened
to the ghost on your shoulder.

CARRY ME GENTLY

Come with me.
Carry me gently,
    as a ghost,
    silenced to the world.
Sleep like the dead and
    awake feeling alive.

Over the window's fall,
my toes on the precipice,
I hemorrhage you,
    loving and hating,
    tearing and soothing,
    by accident,
    by design.

Despair, casting its shadows,
holds the darkness and
leaves me with my past.
I'll rewrite the script and
    live in my words.

Then God and the Devil will
walk away.

ACT II

the forest

pg. 18 - 29

STAY

We are all wounded,
fighting a war no one can see,
clutching a bible filled with
       someone else's dreams,
living off of blood-stained chocolate,
wishing for answers to prayers
       long forgotten…
longing to be free.

I don't know how I got away, but
I walked these fabled roads after
my mama called me home
to this landfill of words and memories.

"Stay here," she said.
"Stay always."

HUMAN

Humans,
>   molded like clay,
>   simple and perverse,
>   decorated in metaphors,
> outlast the immortal,
>   the strong,
>   the holy,
> as though we invented silence.

A WORLD WITHOUT US

The war on poetry:
One word more, one breath less.
We marry the world, and
fall into the sky.
We are the fallen,
waiting for redemption
with words and liquid promises
that turn into lies.
The shape of our words,
they will outlast us.
No one ever taught us to fail
so we drink in the rain.
Show me who you are and
when your wings were clipped
by this disease called society,
a god someone told you to pray to.

Imagine a world without us.

DO YOU REMEMBER IT?

Seduced by your song,
delicate and dangerous,
I yield.
I yield to you.

Do you remember it?
Keeping me enraptured,
submerging me,
kicking me like a bad habit,
loving me like a nightmare
    bleeding on white?
I yielded.
I always yielded to you.

Is the soul immortal?
Will I meet you on the other side?
Don't give me hope.
I will always yield to you.

FIXED IN PLACE

At the end of a journey
for none but a god
over the fathomless dark,
the bare moon by your side
(fixed in place),
quiet in the wasteland kissed by the fog,
sits a dark grave like a drowned effigy.

Enter your heart,
enter your soul.
Goodbye, hope and prayers
(pure and solemn like water),
every bead on a rosary
a prayer unanswered.

The Devil sits beside you,
a king of fools,
carving his next masterpiece.

THORNS OVER PETALS

You've found me in shades of grey.

Let me be lonely,
closer with every lie to
an unborn reality,
gross and unaware,
breathing thoughts,
burning words, and
dreaming of drowning.

You broke me into something good.

But I chose thorns over petals,
a place of surrender,
a safe skin to wear,
an unforgiving hymn.

Burn your tongue with my name and
save your lies for someone that
matters.

ONCE UPON A MISTAKE

"Once upon a mistake" began the
darkest of fairy tales.
With no angel or saint
to guide our way,
I hid you beneath the stars.

You said, "We need another god."

"Damaged goods never wasted, the brethren
of none, the Devil, once an angel, still knows
the music of the heavens."

ONLY THE TREES WILL KNOW

When the lights extinguish,
we are not human.

I am the darkness and the light,
breaking the world into pieces,
my heart an earthquake of
unimaginable tremors,
uttering a language no one speaks.
Twisting the rose petals,
my love is made flesh.

Only the trees will know.

EDEN

Pressured and bound,
flirting with death,
I'll sip your skin.

Making dead promises,
the Devil will take you away to
a forest with no end.

Reaching for dreams,
we lost ourselves to time...

Tie a little ribbon like a noose,
save your dying breath,
and abandon your eyes.

You are my first,
I am your last.

The Devil is a long-lost friend of mine,
and Eden is no longer
home.

CIRCLES

We're running in circles, but
this is our home now.

Awake in an insane world,
nonsense words that mean
   everything
   and
   nothing,
bound together by
   hopes
   and
   dreams,
a slave to
   sensation,
hearts in
   twain,
rules already
   broken,
   twisted
   and
   wonderful,
in a sky of
   flames...

We are home now.

ACT III

the roots

pg. 32- 35

ANNIVERSARY OF A LIFE
LONG FORGOTTEN

On the anniversary of a life long forgotten,
I rush to the altar to kneel,
walking beside its ghosts.

On the anniversary of a life long forgotten,
my name is fragile, so
handle it with care,
strong and slow, push and blow,
so is above, so is below.

On the anniversary of a life long forgotten,
a-tisket, a-tasket,
rain fills up the casket...
but you can't save me.

On the anniversary of a life long forgotten,
every soul sovereign,
close to the feeling of life,
I undo the sun.

On the anniversary of a life long forgotten,
a soul will always find its way home.

THE WORDS I WOULD SAY AT
YOUR FUNERAL

I know the words I would say at your funeral.

Here we are,
living in the illusion of choice,
every fateful encounter
written in stone,
time descending like
drops of rain,
hither and thither and
wither and die.

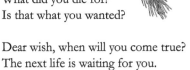

Where were you going?
What did you die for?
Is that what you wanted?

Dear wish, when will you come true?
The next life is waiting for you.
Are you ready for it?

WHAT GOOD HAS IT DONE THE WORLD?

Another lifetime away,
we were no better than
rats and rodents,
making imaginary mountains
that built themselves into
a prison of flames.

Fine as a wilted flower
(and fodder for the heart),
I am
from the moments that made me:
A cold-blooded killer,
a ghost of a soul,
making history.

What good has it done the world?

THANK YOU FOR YOUR CONTRIBUTION

Thank you for your contribution
to the world of the living.
Not of this world
or any other,
a life unlived…

How lucky you are.

Forward in motion,
answering our own questions,
you give us hope,
give us light and
tip the world on its side.

The world doesn't care
that everything that destroys you
blurs the memory of
what we once were,
oh, sepulchre of the dead.

You are a facsimile,
a soul sewn into wax,
but this is our perdition.

Until next we wake.

THANK

This all started with a few strips of paper. When I was at work, I ended up with a pile of cardstock slips and had the strange idea of writing the random phrases that would pop into my head on them for later use. I had no ultimate goal with them, only to get my thoughts down in some form that wasn't complete or unfinished. It evolved into a writing exercise I use to create poems – the paper slips, folded in half and gathered in a bowl, are picked at random to rearrange into some sort of story or narrative on paper. It has invigorated me and expanded my idea of what poetry could be.

I never imagined this concept of narratives constructed through random choice would evolve into so much more, including an art collaboration with my friend and mentor Mari Omori, and eventually this poetry collection. I am grateful this writing journey has taken me down such interesting but familiar paths, uniting many artistic mediums into one multi-faceted experience, much like a forest of trees planting its roots.

YOU

I am extremely grateful to Mari for seeing something artistic in an idea so small; Kris Larson and June Woest for trusting our evolving ideas blindly; Jason Watson for feeding my hobby with way more paper than it'll ever need; and Angie Spargur for giving *The Forest* a second set of eyes it needed to become what you see today.

I couldn't have done this without my husband Jared, who has been a positive and loving support system whether he knew it or not (most likely not); Beth Huston for the wonderful inspirational conversations we've had and believing in my crazy ideas even when I didn't; Riza Press, Tricia Jones, Ava Balis, and everyone who has made Riza the wonderful publisher it is; and my mother Lori and father Guy for cheering me on in the random things I do.

Here's to an ever-expanding universe of crazy ideas and the wonderful people who don't make them sound crazy. We need more people like you in the world.

ABOUT T.C.

find t.c. anderson online:

thetcanderson.com | @thetcanderson

T.C. Anderson is a writer, artist, and multimedia designer with work published in literary journals *Capsule Stories*, *Pages Penned in Pandemic: A Collective*, mental health anthology *Pluviophile*, and more. *The Forest* is her first poetry collection, accompanying an art installation of the same name being developed with artist Mari Omori.

When not writing, Anderson is an award-winning graphic designer at Lone Star College in Kingwood, Texas, currently studying for her Bachelor of Arts in Graphic Design & Media Arts from Southern New Hampshire University. She lives in Houston with her husband Jared and their furbaby Boomer.

CPSIA information can be obtained
at www.ICGtesting.com
Printed in the USA
BVHW061128040521
606425BV00012B/2909